EZINE KALEIDOSCOPE NOVEMBER 2024

THE JOURNEY WITHIN - 14TH ANNIVERSARY EDITION

EZINE KALEIDOSCOPE

Made with ♥ on the Notion Press Platform
www.notionpress.com

Contents

I

From the Editor's Desk

Dear Reader,

This November, we proudly celebrate the 14th anniversary of Ezine Kaleidoscope. When we launched in 2010, our vision was to create a space for writers to share their voices and bring content that delves into the softer side of life. Over the years, our journey has evolved, and so has our magazine. Today, Ezine Kaleidoscope stands as a beacon of personal growth and spirituality.

Yet, there was a time when something felt missing. As we continued to grow and expand our vision, the magazine went dormant for a couple of years. But with time and reflection, clarity emerged. We realized that there is a significant gap in how spirituality is perceived—a gap between daily life and the deeper essence of our spiritual selves. Spirituality is often seen as a separate aspect of life, neatly compartmentalized and kept apart.

We tend to forget that we are not merely humans experiencing a spiritual journey; we are spiritual beings navigating a human journey. It is our connection to our spiritual selves that serves as a reliable compass, guiding us through life's challenges and helping us find our true path.

And so, Ezine Kaleidoscope transformed, embracing the idea of practical spirituality. Our mission became clear—to bridge the gap between everyday life and spiritual wisdom, to bring insights that make spirituality accessible, and to inspire a holistic way of living.

This November 2024, we invite you to join us in celebrating this transformative journey. Our theme for this anniversary edition is "The Journey Within." Within these pages, you will discover stories of individuals who have embarked on their unique spiritual paths, exploring the many facets of personal and spiritual growth. Because, in the end, life itself is a journey—a journey within.

You will also discover the aspect of the journey in healing, chakras and the concept of Zine itself. Thank you for being a part of our community, and we look forward to many more years of growth and exploration together.

With grace and light,

Meetu Sehgal
Editor/Founder
Ezine Kaleidoscope

II

The Unfiltered Voice of Zines: Evolution of Self-Expression with Art Therapy

The Unfiltered
Voice of Zines:
Evolution of Self-Expression
with Art Therapy

Whether you have been exploring *Kaleidoscope* for a while now or you are encountering it for the first time, you may have paused to wonder- why is it called an "Ezine"? While it might seem obvious that it stands for "Electronic Zine," there is a much deeper story behind the word "zine" itself. On the occasion of the 14th anniversary of Kaleidoscope Ezine, we invite you to dive into the fascinating world of zines and uncover the rich culture and history that has shaped this unique form of expression.

Zines, short for fanzines or magazines, have a long and rich history as a form of self-expression, dating back to the early 20th century. The origins of zines are often traced to the **science fiction** fan communities of the 1930s. Early sci-fi enthusiasts began publishing their own "fanzines" to share opinions, reviews, and fan-written stories, giving birth to the zine movement. It signifies something much more intimate and DIY. Zines were never intended for mass production. Instead, they allowed creators to directly speak to small, specific audiences. In the early days, these publications were usually photocopied or mimeographed and distributed by hand, through the mail, or at fan conventions. These early fanzines bypassed traditional publishing, offering grassroots alternatives for fans to connect and engage with niche topics that mainstream media often ignored.

In the 1970s, punk culture embraced zines as a way to spread messages of rebellion, DIY ethos, and alternative viewpoints. Over the decades, zines have grown into a powerful medium for self-expression, activism, creative freedom and healing, finding their place in subcultures, political movements, and personal narratives.

Zines in the Punk and Counterculture Movements

Zines truly exploded in the 1970s, during the rise of the **punk subculture**. The DIY ethos of punk music extended to zine-making, with fans and musicians alike producing zines that documented the raw, rebellious energy of the scene. Iconic punk zines like *Sniffin' Glue* (UK) and *Maximumrocknroll* (USA) captured the spirit of underground music, offering a space for anti-establishment ideas and unfiltered self-expression.

During this time, zines became a vital medium for countercultures, offering marginalised groups a platform to critique mainstream society, voice political dissent, and explore alternative lifestyles. The beauty of zines was that anyone could make one—there were no gatekeepers. This gave rise to amplification of zines on topics like **feminism**, **queer identity**, and

anarchism, creating communities around these underground publications.

The Riot Grrrl Movement and Feminist Zines

In the 1990s, zines took on a new level of cultural significance within the **Riot Grrrl** movement. Emerging from the punk scene, Riot Grrrl was a feminist movement that used music, art, and zines to protest issues like sexism, sexual violence, and body image. Iconic zines such as *Bikini Kill*, produced by the band of the same name, tackled feminist topics head-on and inspired countless young women to take up the medium as a tool of resistance and empowerment.

Riot Grrrl zines became a vehicle for feminist solidarity, offering a safe space for women and girls to explore their identities and speak out against oppression. This wave of zines also helped carve out a space for marginalised voices in a male-dominated punk scene.

Zines in the Digital Age

With the rise of the internet in the 2000s, the zine culture adapted to the digital world. E-zines (electronic zines) emerged, allowing creators to publish and distribute their work online. While the internet made zines more accessible to a global audience, it also transformed the traditional zine-making process. E-zines embraced the DIY ethos of print zines but offered more reach and immediacy. However, physical zines never lost their appeal, as many creators and readers continue to value the tactile, handmade nature of printed zines.

Today, zines have diversified in form and content. They cover an array of topics, from personal memoirs to activism, art, mental health, politics, and identity. Contemporary zine culture is a global phenomenon, with zine fairs, festivals, and workshops held worldwide, connecting zine makers and readers from different cultures and backgrounds.

In an age dominated by social media, digital platforms, and instant gratification, one might think that physical, DIY publications like zines would be a thing of the past. However, Millennials and Gen Z are rediscovering and reimagining zine culture, making it more relevant than ever. Far from fading into obscurity, zines have become a powerful medium of expression, activism, and even spirituality for these generations, blending old-school DIY ethos with modern digital tools.

The Use and Power of Zines

Zines have always been a medium of empowerment, giving voice to the voiceless. Their low-cost production makes them accessible to creators who lack the resources or interest in mainstream publishing. Zines can be as simple or as intricate as the creator desires, allowing for limitless creativity. Zines are experiencing a renaissance among Millennials (born roughly between 1981 and 1996) and Gen Z (born between 1997 and 2012) for a number of reasons:

Zines as Activism

Zines are often used as tools for activism, providing a platform to discuss radical politics, protest movements, and social justice causes. They've been instrumental in amplifying marginalised voices. This has only intensified with Millennials and Gen Z. Both generations are known for their political engagement and desire for social change and critique systemic issues. From climate change and racial justice to feminism and LGBTQ+ rights, zines are being used to address the pressing social issues of today, offering a platform that is uncensored, radical, and unapologetic. Millennials and Gen Z have grown up witnessing the rise of corporate monopolies, the commodification of creativity, and the commercialization of nearly every aspect of life. For many, zines represent a break from capitalist systems of media and art production. They embody the DIY (do-it-yourself) ethos, where anyone can create without needing large budgets, corporate backing, or editorial approval. This aligns with the younger generations' preference for authenticity over polished, commercialised content.

Zines as a Rebellion Against Digital Overload

In an increasingly digital world, there's a growing desire among younger generations to engage in offline, hands-on activities. Zines offer a tangible, analogue experience just like a podcast, that feels intimate and personal-qualities that are often missing in the fast-paced world of Instagram, TikTok, and YouTube. Creating and reading a physical zine allows individuals to step away from the screen, connect with their creativity, and produce something tangible that can be held and shared in the real world.

Zines as Art

Many zines are works of art in themselves, combining writing, photography, collage, illustration, and graphic design. They allow artists to experiment with form and content without the constraints of traditional publishing or art galleries. This art-centred approach to zines has fostered a vibrant underground community of visual and literary artists. The resurgence of zine-making is also tied to the love for nostalgia and vintage aesthetics among younger generations. Millennials, in particular, experienced the tail end of the pre-internet era, while Gen Z has grown up in a world saturated by technology. Both generations have a fascination with "vintage" formats – vinyl records, Polaroid cameras, and now zines. They offer an escape from the digital world. Zines carry a certain retro appeal, harking back to the days of punk and riot grrrl movements, which adds to their allure.

Zines as Personal Expression

For many, zines are deeply personal. They serve as journals, diaries, or memoirs, allowing the creator to explore their identity, emotions, or experiences. Many zines are deeply intimate, created not for commercial gain but as a way of working through personal issues or documenting unique perspectives. Authenticity is highly valued by both Millennials and Gen Z, who often find mainstream media to be overly curated and inauthentic. Zines, with their unpolished, raw style, offer a platform for genuine self-expression. Unlike social media, which often promotes a curated version of reality, zines allow creators to explore messy, unfiltered ideas and emotions. The personal, handmade quality of zines gives them an authenticity that resonates deeply with younger creators and readers.

Zines as Community Builders

Zines are also community builders. They offer a sense of belonging and solidarity to those who feel excluded from mainstream culture. Zine fairs and festivals (more on this later) provide spaces for like-minded creators and readers to come together, share ideas, and support one another.

Zines for Spiritual Exploration and Healing

Beyond activism and self-expression, zines have also become a powerful tool for spiritual exploration and healing, especially among younger generations who are moving away from traditional organised religion and toward more personal, eclectic spiritual practices. Millennials and Gen Z have embraced spirituality in many forms like meditation, energy healing, astrology, tarot, and witchcraft. They have started seeing them as tools for personal growth and self-discovery. Zines have become a natural extension of this spiritual journey, offering creators and readers alike a space to reflect on their spiritual practices, share rituals, and explore metaphysical topics.

Many zines, just like Kaleidoscope, are now dedicated to themes like **crystal healing**, **astrology**, **tarot reading**, **manifestation practices**, and **chakras**. These spiritual zines often combine text, imagery, and symbols to create a sacred experience for the reader. By exploring the intersection of creativity and spirituality, zine-makers are creating powerful tools for mindfulness, reflection, and healing. For those who value authenticity, connection, and self-expression, zines offer a deeply personal way to engage with their spiritual selves.

Global Significance of Zines

Zines are not confined to any one country or culture. They are truly a global phenomenon, with diverse zine scenes thriving across the world.

In North America, the zine culture is strongly linked to the punk and underground music scenes, as well as feminist, anarchist, and queer movements. The U.S. and Canada host some of the most well-known zine fests, such as the **Brooklyn Zine Fest**, **Chicago Zine Fest**, and **Portland Zine Symposium**.

In the UK and Europe, zines have long been connected to political activism, particularly around anti-fascism, anti-racism, and anarchism. European zine culture is vast, with many cities holding zine fairs and encouraging the DIY art movement.

Latin America has a thriving zine culture, often connected to resistance against political oppression and the exploration of indigenous identity and feminism. Countries like Mexico, Brazil, and Argentina have zine makers who use their work to critique authoritarian regimes, colonialism, and gender-based violence.

In Asia, zine culture is also flourishing. In Japan, zines (referred to as *doujinshi*) have strong ties to the anime and manga subcultures. Zine-making is also growing in countries like India and Indonesia, where young creators use zines to express their views on identity, politics, and art in societies often governed by culture, tradition and conformity.

In India, zines are becoming a popular medium among artists and activists alike. Zine makers explore a variety of topics, including feminism, mental health, sexuality, and environmentalism. The rise of events like the **Bombay Zine Fest** and independent collectives focused on zine-making indicates the growing importance of zine culture in India's urban landscape.

The Continued Relevance of Zines

Zines remain relevant because they offer a powerful alternative to mainstream media and publishing. In an age where digital algorithms and corporate interests often dictate what we consume, zines provide a refreshing break from commercialised content. They encourage readers to engage with ideas and voices that may otherwise be overlooked.

For creators, zines represent freedom from the constraints of editors, publishers, and advertisers. Zines are a space for authenticity, where the creator's voice remains unfiltered. They are a testament to the enduring power of DIY culture and the belief that anyone, regardless of resources or background, can create something meaningful.

In essence, zines have grown from humble beginnings in sci-fi fandoms to become a powerful global movement. Their significance lies not just in their content, but in their ability to democratise art, literature, and activism, allowing people to create, express, and connect across the world.

In expressive arts therapy, zines offer a unique platform for individuals to explore their inner worlds, externalise emotions, and channel creative energy in a non-judgmental and intimate format. The flexibility and low cost of zine-making make it a therapeutic tool accessible to everyone, allowing individuals to delve into personal topics at their own pace and through their own lens. By integrating visual art, writing, and collage, zines provide a holistic approach to healing and can serve as a safe container for personal storytelling.

The Healing Power of Zines in Art Therapy

Zines serve as a medium for reflection and self-expression, making them highly effective in addressing various emotional and psychological issues, particularly in the context of healing the chakras. Chakras are energy centres in the body, and when they are blocked, it can affect both physical and emotional well-being.

1. **Sacral Chakra** (Svadhisthana) - Located just below the navel, the sacral chakra governs creativity, sexuality, and emotional flow. Creating zines offers a creative outlet, helping individuals access their creativity and address emotions they may be holding onto. The process of cutting, pasting, drawing, and expressing personal thoughts can be particularly soothing for the sacral chakra, enabling a healthy flow of energy.
2. **Throat Chakra** (Vishuddha) - The throat chakra is the centre of communication and self-expression. Zine-making encourages individuals to share their thoughts and feelings in a tangible form, making it a perfect tool for those struggling to verbalise their emotions. Whether through writing, drawing, or simply using images and symbols, zines can help open up this chakra and foster healthy communication.
3. **Third Eye Chakra** (Ajna) - The third eye chakra is associated with intuition and insight. The intuitive nature of zine-making, where there are no strict rules or guidelines, helps stimulate the third eye chakra. As individuals put together their zine, they can tap into their inner wisdom and allow unconscious thoughts to surface, leading to deeper self-awareness and healing.

Mental health awareness has become a central concern for the population of all walks of life, with many seeking alternative forms of therapy, self-expression and well-being. Zines offer a therapeutic outlet for exploring feelings of anxiety, depression, isolation, and personal trauma. In fact, many zines are dedicated entirely to the subject of mental health, offering a space for creators to share their struggles and coping mechanisms. These personal zines provide comfort to readers who may feel isolated in their experiences, fostering a sense of solidarity and collective healing.

For example, many Gen Z creators have used zines to chronicle their experiences with the COVID-19 pandemic, turning their anxiety, uncertainty, and loneliness into creative expression. In this sense, zines serve not only as a tool for personal catharsis but also as a way to document and make sense of global events.

Simple DIY Zine-Making Guide (A4 Size Sheet)

Materials Needed:

- A4 size sheet of paper
- Scissors
- Pens, markers, or coloured pencils
- Glue stick or tape
- Magazines or printed images for collage
- Optional: stickers, washi tape, colours, fabric, or any other decorative materials

Step-by-Step Guide to Make a Simple Zine:

1. **Fold the Paper**:

   - Take the A4 sheet and fold it in half vertically (hotdog style).
   - Open it back up and fold it in half horizontally (hamburger style).
   - Fold it in half again horizontally, so you end up with 8 small rectangular sections.

2. **Cut the Center**:

   - Unfold the paper and lay it flat.
   - Using scissors, make a small cut along the centrefold from the middle of the page to the first fold. This will create an opening in the middle of the paper.

3. **Fold into a Zine Shape**:

   - Refold the paper in half horizontally. Then, hold the paper on both ends and gently push the two ends toward each other until the paper forms a cross shape.

- Fold the paper into a booklet by folding the cross sections onto one another.

4. **Create Your Content**:

- Begin adding your artwork, drawings, or writing on each of the 8 pages of the zine. You can use markers, pens, or coloured pencils to decorate. Feel free to add collaged images, textures, and cutouts to express your ideas.

5. **Theme-Based Pages**:

- For zine art focused on healing chakras, you can dedicate each page to a different aspect of your emotional healing. For example:

  - Page 1: Title of the zine
  - Page 2: Root Chakra (Muladhara) – Grounding and Stability. Red, symbolising stability, strength, and survival.
  - Page 3: Sacral Chakra (Svadhisthana) – Creativity and Emotional Flow. Orange, symbolising joy, pleasure, and creativity.
  - Page 4: Solar Plexus Chakra (Manipura) – Personal Power and Confidence. Yellow, representing inner strength, willpower, and vitality
  - Page 5: Heart Chakra (Anahata) – Love and Compassion. Green and pink, symbolising love, balance, and emotional healing.
  - Page 6: Throat Chakra (Vishuddha) – Expression and Communication. Blue, symbolising clarity, communication, and authenticity.
  - Page 7: Third Eye Chakra (Ajna) – Intuition and Insight. Indigo, symbolising insight, imagination, and clarity of mind.
  - Pages 8: Crown Chakra (Sahasrara) – Connection to the Divine. Violet or white, symbolising purity, oneness, and connection to the universe.
  - Additional page(Optional to add): A reflection or closing statement. Rainbow or any combination of the seven chakra colours of your choice.

6. **Personalise and Share**:

   - Once you have filled your zine, feel free to photocopy it to share with others or simply keep it as a personal healing tool. You can always go back to your zines for reviewing personal lessons and reflecting upon your emotions.

Techniques to Make Your Zine Unique:

- **Doodle and Sketch**: Use simple sketches or some doodles that represent how you feel. Don't worry about perfect drawing. let the process be intuitive. It is not for the world to see and judge. It is for you.
- **Collage Art**: Collect images, colours, or words that resonate with your current emotional state or healing journey, and create a collage to represent different aspects of your life.
- **Free Writing**: Use stream-of-consciousness writing to express thoughts, emotions, or dreams related to your chakras or just whatever comes to your mind.
- **Poems:** You can write your own poems if you are a poet or prefer expressing through poetry.
- **Colour Therapy**: Incorporate colours associated with each chakra (e.g., orange for sacral, blue for throat, and indigo for third eye) to add a layer of energy work to your zine.

Indian Zine Artists to Explore

India has a rich and emerging zine culture, with artists using this medium to express themselves on topics such as identity, politics, mental health, and personal stories.

Priya Daliwal – Viral Dreams

- Zine Theme: Priya's zine Viral Dreams explores themes of isolation, connection, and dreamscapes during the COVID-19 pandemic. Her zine blends personal narratives, poetry, and surreal illustrations, reflecting the emotional turbulence of the time while emphasising healing and introspection.

- Style: Her work often includes hand-drawn sketches combined with digital art, creating a dreamy, ethereal visual aesthetic.

Aparna Nair – Queer Chronicles

- Zine Theme: Queer Chronicles by Aparna Nair is a zine focusing on LGBTQ+ stories, especially in the context of Indian society. It highlights issues related to identity, gender, and sexuality, told through personal essays, interviews, and vibrant illustrations.
- Style: Aparna uses a blend of collage, photography, and bold typography to capture the rawness and authenticity of queer narratives.

Shreyas R. Krishnan – Specimens of Absence

- Zine Theme: Shreyas's zine Specimens of Absence focuses on memory, loss, and the passage of time. The zine includes delicate, hand-drawn botanical illustrations juxtaposed with reflections on the ephemeral nature of existence, inviting readers to meditate on absence and presence in their lives.
- Style: Known for her intricate line work and minimalist design, Shreyas incorporates nature elements into her work, often symbolising emotional depth and introspection.

With just a few simple steps, anyone can create their own zine and embark on a journey of self-expression and healing. Happy Zineing!

You are welcome to join an upcoming zine workshop with me. Share your zines on Instagram and tag @Ezine Kaleidoscope and @gogetteraashi on Instagram. We would love to see your creations.

About the Writer

Ashi Sharma

Ashi Sharma is a multi-faceted professional and an inspiring force in the realms of personal development and holistic healing. As an author, expressive arts therapy practitioner, EFT practitioner, tarot healer, and podcaster at Breaking Mythos, she brings a unique blend of insights to her work as a Reiki master, lifestyle and business coach and consultant. She has been honoured in the BW Wellbeing World 30 Under 30 Awards for the years 2022 and 2023. Her latest work is part of a beautiful coffee table book, 'Mythology' enriched with hand-painted illustrations that bring ancient stories and legends to life. In this book, she talks about the spiritual journeys of Shukracharya and Odin.

III

Understanding the Healing Journey: Stages and Challenges

Understanding
the Healing Journey:
Stages and Challenges

Healing is supposed to be a journey that makes you feel good. Right? Yes, but!

The feeling good happens once you have journeyed through feeling the highs and lows of life, messy emotions, negative beliefs and patterns, unlearning and re-learning things and so on. And this process can end up feeling like an uphill journey with seemingly no end.

When my clients ask me, "When will I be healed completely?", sadly the answer to this is "I don't know". But what I do know is that it gets better over time. It doesn't feel this messy after having done some work on yourself and having healed yourself.

The toughest part of the healing journey is getting started. Most people get started on their healing journey when they go through a painful experience – failed relationship, heartbreak, financial loss, health problems – and they find themselves in a corner. I don't want to use the word hopeless here, but that's what it is.

The journey within of healing is one of the toughest journeys one can ever take and yet be the most rewarding.

What is the meaning of healing?

Whether it's a physical health issue, an emotional issue, a financial/business problem, or a relationship problem, the problem or an issue indicates there is some energy imbalance in the person's energy system.

We are not just physical bodies that you see, we are much more than that. We are energy beings, made of energy, run on energy and dissolve into energy.

In the Bhagavad Gita Lord Krishna talks about this:

> "**Bhagavad Gita 7.4 (Sanskrit):**bhūmir āpo 'nalo vāyuḥ khaṁ mano buddhir eva ca | ahaṅkāra itīyaṁ me bhinnā prakṛtir aṣṭadhā ||"

In this verse, Lord Krishna explains that the elements of nature, including the physical body, are manifestations of His energies. "Water, earth, air, fire, ether, mind, intelligence, and false ego - they are My energies". What is your body? This external body - that is your energy.

Your body is made out of your energy. Your whole life is made of energy vibrations, created by your subconscious desires and programs embedded deep within the unconscious.

This is also what the Law of Attraction states.

This means that when energies are in harmony, you will experience ease and flow in life. When the energies are not in harmony, you will experience dis-ease and problems.

Healing essentially means bringing the energies into harmony, this helps your body and mind heal itself.

So, whether it is physical healing or emotional healing, healing relationships or finances, it is all about bringing the energies into harmony.

This can be done through energy healing like Reiki, Pranic healing, Angelic healing, etc. It can also be done by new-age therapeutic methods like EFT (Emotional Freedom Technique), NLP (Neuro-Linguistic Programming), etc. It can also be done through practicing meditation and building awareness. Each of these methods has its strengths and can be used in combination as well.

So, what is the journey of healing like? What will happen? What to expect?

No matter what kind of healing you are doing and what method(s) you are using, the healing is likely to go through some stages.

Stage 1: Awareness

All healing begins with the awareness that something needs to be healed, that something is not working. Your emotions usually are the best compass for you that guide you into becoming aware of the problem or the fact that there is some problem that needs to be addressed.

So often, we keep going through life, carrying the burdens of our problems with no awareness of the fact that without these burdens, our lives can become so much easier. And then, many times we feel that there is no solution to these burdens and that they will always be there.

Usually, this happens to most people when they are at the lowest points in their life and can't see any way up. This is when you are experiencing pain, distress or grief.

What is really lacking here is the perspective.

A little bit of shift in perspective can help us see that one doesn't have to carry these burdens necessarily, or that what you are looking at as burdens are, in fact, opportunities in disguise. And healing can help you deal with this in a more efficient and easier manner.

A willingness to look at things with awareness can kick-start your healing journey.

Stage 2: Acceptance and Surrender

The next step is accepting what is. It also involves accepting what is not working.

There is a saying, "What we resist persists, what we accept can change."

It requires allowing yourself to feel what you are feeling fully, moving through the discomfort and dropping the judgment or resistance, if any. This is also accompanied by surrender.

Surrender doesn't mean giving up, on the contrary, it means becoming open to help and healing. So often our egos don't allow us to acknowledge what's wrong. The belief systems that do not let us surrender can look something like "It's not ok to make mistakes", "If something is wrong, it means I am a failure", or "It's not ok to be vulnerable".

Fortunately or unfortunately, Suffering and pain usually help us accept and surrender to the healing process.

Once we accept and make peace with what is, the body can finally relax and begin to heal.

Stage 3: Processing

This is also the exploration phase. This is the stage when you actively begin to heal and explore underlying emotions, root causes, and the history of when and where it started. This is the stage of addressing unresolved trauma, wading through the waters of old beliefs and emotions, and processing the uncomfortable emotions and memories.

Processing doesn't mean diving into memories and ruminating and feeling bad. It means healing the emotions and beliefs formed in those events. This can happen through self-reflection, journaling, EFT, expressive arts therapy or working with a good therapist.

Stage 4: Release

The release is often about facing your emotions, fears, painful past and completing stories. This is a time that can be accompanied by waterworks and feeling tender and vulnerable.

This is the time when you start to experience some progress in your healing journey. Your triggers don't trigger you as much. Life begins to look better and a little easier. Many surface layers of problems are healed.

You begin to experience freedom and ease in the way life happens to you.

Stage 5: Apparent Relapse

This is the time when the roller coaster journey of healing begins. As one layer heals, more stuff from the subconscious begins to surface. You start to unravel emotions, beliefs and patterns that you have been running in your life.

At this stage, it might feel like you are back to square one and all progress has been for nothing. But that's not true.

What is really happening is that as you heal some things and that layer is peeled, the next layer begins to show up. So although it may seem like there has been no progress, the truth is that you have evolved and are ready to heal deeper issues and layers.

Think of it as peeling the layers of an onion. You keep peeling and with every peeling, some tears also accompany the process until there is nothing left to peel.

Stage 6: Growth

This process continues for some until the intensity of layers and issues begins to reduce and the triggers don't trigger you as much as they used to. At this point, it may seem like a never-ending journey. But the intensity of triggers becomes less.

This is the time when you begin to notice progress in different areas of life – the ones where you were healing and even the ones where you were not.

You derive lessons and wisdom from the past events and pain, your awareness increases, you find yourself evolving into a new being.

Stage 7: Integration

This stage feels like a rebirth and is accompanied by rediscovering yourself in this new phase of life. The old no longer sticks, the new is not yet here. You are in a state of flux, trying to understand new ways to deal with life, people and situations.

You are integrating the lessons and wisdom into your new being. You start to show up differently in your relationships. This is the time when you need to have patience with your loved ones as they adjust to the new you.

Your choices and perspectives also shift, and you begin to attract a new tribe of people as well who resonate with this new you. You feel more confident in your ability to handle life, more resilient and wise and more aware in your present life.

Summing up the Journey

This journey of healing through the 7 stages happens for everyone. Each individual takes their own time traversing the stages. It is possible to get stuck in one stage for a longer period of time as compared to others.

Healing is always a one-step forward and two-step back journey. It can sometimes feel that you are going backwards or are stagnant in one place for a long time, but once you reach the stage of Growth, then there is no going backwards.

The journey may not be the same for everyone, one may jump back and forth through the stages, but more or less, the journey keeps happening at its own pace. It takes courage and willingness to take this journey but the rewards at the end are worth making it.

About the Writer

Meetu Sehgal

Meetu Sehgal is a Personal Transformation and Emotional Wellness Coach, EFT Trainer, Tarot Reader, Author, Reiki Grandmaster and Counselling Psychologist. With more than 15 years of experience in her field, she has been passionately working with individuals, helping them resolve health, wealth and relationship challenges through coaching. Meetu Sehgal is an MBA graduate from Delhi University and also holds a Masters in Psychology. Passionate about writing and spirituality, she has blended both in her work, which has helped hundreds of people around the world find peace within themselves. Her latest book, "Happy Inside Out", is a definitive guide to understanding and handling emotions and moods.

IV

Exploring the Root Chakra: Foundation of Energy and Emotional Stability

Exploring
the Root Chakra:
Foundation of Energy
and Emotional Stability

The concept of Aura and Chakras seems like common knowledge these days, compared to a decade or two ago when most people were not familiar with the energy concept. It is even used by Westerners in their books related to holistic healing and living.

The concept of Chakras stems from Indian philosophy, tantra and yoga. The word "Chakra" literally means "disk" or "wheel" in Sanskrit and refers to different energy centres in the subtle human body. There are many Chakras but the ones we most often talk or hear about are the seven major Chakras that run up our body along with the spine. They start with the root Chakra at the base of the spine and extend to the crown Chakra, located at the top of our head.

It has long been believed that we have both a physical body and a subtle body. This concept was later supported by Kirlian photography, which captures images of our aura. The physical and subtle bodies are thought to exist in parallel dimensions. The physical body is located in the physical world that we can see with our physical eyes. The energy or subtle body is connected by energy pathways (or channels) known as nadis (energy meridians). According to Vigyan Bhairav Tantra, there are 72000 nadis. These nadis are connected and directed by nodes of psychic energy known as Chakras.

The physical body can affect the energy body and vice versa. Each of the seven major Chakras has different physical and psychological effects on our body, meaning that an unbalanced chakra has a particular effect on our body and mind.

To start the balancing process, one should ideally start from the base chakra as the kundalini energy, also known as the coiled serpent power sleeping in the Muladhara chakra, moves from the base upwards towards the crown for the purpose of activation of the psychic power.

Understanding the Muladhara (The Root Chakra)

The word "Muladhara " in Sanskrit means "root " hence, its English name. The Muladhara, or the Root Chakra, is located at the base of the spine.

Muladhara – the Foundation

This chakra acts as the root of your body and is linked to the element earth. It is believed that the whole universe, as well as our body, is made of five elements called **Panch Mahabhoots** that are earth, air, fire, water and ether.

The root chakra is the base or foundation. I have met many meditators who mainly focus on concentrating on the third eye chakra to awaken powers, but they gain it only for a short period of time, as they forget to work on the root or other lower chakras first. This is like a multistorey building without a strong foundation, which can collapse anytime. For a durable building, a strong foundation is a must.

Similarly, the Muladhara chakra acts as the root of your body and is associated with the earth element, which represents a person's ability to feel rooted, grounded and stable in life. It is connected to family relationships and a sense of security. If your root chakra is healthy you feel confident, safe and secure in life This chakra supports your bone structure and your connection with the physical world around you. If the root chakra is blocked or unbalanced, the other chakras are also affected.

The yogic texts talk about the three main nadis – Ida, Pingala, and Sushmana – that emerge from the root chakra.

Each chakra is associated with a deity as well. Lord Ganpati is associated with the root chakra. Lord Ganpati is the deity who brings good luck and removes obstacles from life.

The root chakra is where everything in your body begins. It is the home of your emotions. An unbalanced root chakra will lead to swings in your emotional state. Other symptoms include feelings of anger, insecurity, restlessness, fear, panic and anxiety, which your body sees as a threat to your safety and security.

This chakra is also related to Karma. You carry not only your experiences but also ancestral memories, generational luck, and trauma in this chakra. So, healing and balancing the root will also balance the Karma.

Symptoms of Weak or Unbalanced Root Chakra

In the 25 years of my healing career, I have seen some patterns and symptoms of a weak root charka.

- Those who have had negative personal struggles such as trouble with their financial situation, job, career, interpersonal relationships and worries about ensuring their survival needs.

- Because of its location at the base of the spine, specifically in the pelvic region, it also impacts sexuality and sex life. Therefore, people with imbalanced root chakra may be afraid of intimacy or have trust issues in relationships.
- Several physical and emotional problems can be prevalent in the lower body, like weight gain or weight loss, problems with the colon and bladder, problems in the lower leg or feet, pain in the lower back, prostrate problems in men, and weakened immunity.
- The other psychological and emotional symptoms are depression, lack of confidence and self-esteem, fear of loss, erratic behaviour, feeling lethargic, etc.

A balanced root chakra shows a healthy survival instinct and a sense of belonging with the people around, grounded and secure. I have seen clients with unbalanced root chakra always feel lack and focus on the negative side even though they are in a good position in comparison to others.

While reading this, you may do a self-assessment and recognise people having weak root chakra just by the symptoms mentioned here.

Ways to Heal and Balance the Root Chakra

The universe has all the solutions. Our chakras are constantly interacting with the thoughts and energy around us. If someone wishes to heal and balance one's chakra, there are many methods like yoga, meditation crystal healing, aromatherapy and much more.

Some of the techniques to help you balance your root chakra are:

Watch what you think: Stop feeding negative thoughts and replace your thoughts with something positive.

Gratitude: Count your blessings and be grateful for what you have instead of cribbing.

Engage with Nature: As root chakra is associated with the earth, engage with nature to strengthen your earth element. This can be walking barefoot on grass, spending time in the garden, or plants in your balcony, gardening, or dancing.

Affirmations: You can also chant affirmations like mantras. For instance, I am safe, I am healthy and full of life, I am one with the earth, The world is my home, The universe is taking care of me.

Working with Breath and Chi: You can start with anulom vilom pranayam practice or tai chi to harmonize your energies.

Crystals: You can wear crystals, carry them with you, or keep them around you. Crystals related to root chakra are Garnet, Hematite, Black Obsidian, Red Jasper, Bloodstone, Smoky quartz, etc.

Essential oils: Essential oils for root chakra healing are cedar, frankincense, sandalwood, patchouli etc.

Professional Help: If you need support you can also seek help from alternative healing such as receiving Reiki healing in person or distance healing, taking EFT sessions in person or online. You can also take access bar sessions to speed up the healing process along with daily remedies.

Worship: You can also request Lord Ganesha to resolve your issues and chant/listen to Ganesha mantras daily.

Meditation: Watch your thoughts and watch your breath. You can also practice the **Grounding Meditation.**

i. Find a quiet place and sit in a comfortable position. Close your eyes
ii. Bring your focus on your root chakra at the base of your spine.
iii. Visualise your favourite tree or any tree if you don't have a favourite tree.
iv. Imagine the roots of the tree growing from your root chakra
v. Inhale and exhale slowly and deeply, feeling grounded and connected to the Earth
vi. Each time you breathe in and out, imagine yourself letting go of the things you don't need or that don't benefit you.
vii. Imagine these things moving down to the trunk of the tree and being released into the Earth beneath you.
viii. Each time you breathe in, imagine your body being nourished
ix. Repeat the inhalation and exhalation while visualising the above-mentioned thought experiment 5 to 10 times.
x. Feel the earth beneath you supporting and embracing you.
xi. When you feel like coming back, slowly open your eyes.

The key is to be consistent with your practice and continue it for at least a few months to truly experience its benefits.

About the Writer

Prathma

Prathma is an expert in various methods of "Wellbeing and Alternative Healing" Modalities. She has been practising & teaching Reiki & other healing Modalities since 1999. A teacher of love and self-acceptance, she brings light and optimism to anyone who meets her. She believes in a holistic approach with a combination and different healing modalities where intuition and logic, science and spirituality go hand-in-hand. Her simplicity and expertise makes the techniques work like powerful charms that have been helping thousands of people around the globe.

V

Love and Limits: How to Set Boundaries Without Building Walls

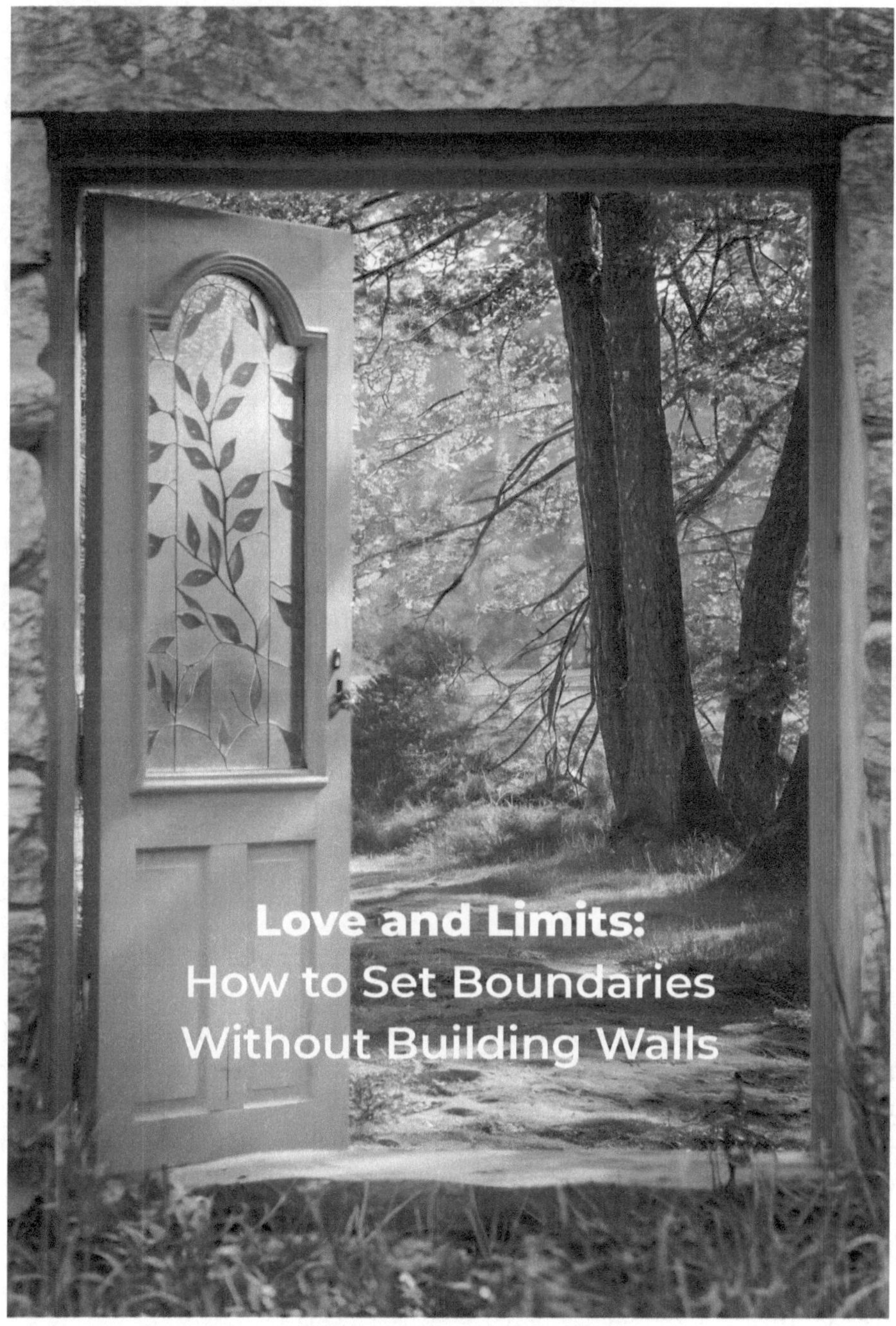
Love and Limits:
How to Set Boundaries
Without Building Walls

Someone once told me boundaries were like a door to a beautiful garden. While this door can be opened and closed, it is up to the owner of this beautiful garden who they wish to let in and who they don't. Perhaps this comparison got stuck in my head for a very simple reason – I have always imagined the concept of boundaries to be a wall that no one can cross. This had always made it difficult to establish boundaries with everyone around me, especially my loved ones.

Why?

Well, why would I want to have walls between me and my friends, family members or even my partner? If I put up walls, how will they enter? How will I communicate what's going on? Or even vice versa?

As I was pondering over this beautiful garden simile where the garden represented my energy, presence, communication and all that I have to offer, the doorbell rang. I knew it was time to start putting things I had just learnt into action.

'Hey Samara! I was wondering..' She pushed her way inside my house and started looking everywhere. 'I was wondering, if maybe you have...'

I was taken aback by her initial rude gesture of welcoming herself into my house but before I could even process that, she made her way into the kitchen to grab things from the counter.

'I don't think you would mind if I just borrowed some ginger and cinnamon. Actually, my daughter Mira is making a new recipe and...'

She suddenly saw a pack of baking soda and instantly took it as if she didn't, I wouldn't let her.

'I'm sorry I think I just realised Mira might need some baking soda too for the recipe.'

'Emm..sure..I guess..' I couldn't manage anything else to come out of my mouth other than that.

I used to think neighbours are good people. Perhaps a bit too naive of me to think that way? Well, they have always been there to help me. My neighbours, I mean.

They check on me when I'm sick, feed me when I'm not well enough to cook and they also... well... That's it, I guess.

But I mean, isn't that a lot anyway?

Feeding people and taking care of a sick person?

And so, yes, I let her get away with everything she took, including the milk bottle from the fridge and then some more stuff.

Maybe she'll return my stuff.

Maybe...

The problem wasn't that she took things because she needed them. The problem was that she didn't even ask, or even promise to return my groceries when she goes out to the market. I mean, she can go out and just buy everything. Or perhaps even order for it to be delivered to her place.

Something didn't feel right.

I know it was just groceries.

Just groceries.

But no, it wasn't about *that*.

It was the attitude that got me. As she was about to set foot out my door, I stopped her.

'*No, don't do it!*' screamed something inside me. '*Just let it go. It's just a few things. Let her have it. Let's have some peace.*'

Peace?

I wonder where did that come from?

My heart raced as her eyes widened to stare blank at my face and then back at her forearm where I held her.

'Emm actually, I need the ginger. For my tea tomorrow morning.' I grabbed it back.

'Also, the milk for the smoothie I'm planning to make.' I grabbed it back too.

'I need that too for this fusion food I want to have with the smoothie.' I took everything back.

She didn't know what to say. She didn't think it would happen. Me stopping her like that. Grabbing her arm and taking everything I bought the night before when I was returning home after extra work hours. I needed the money. It isn't like I haven't shared anything with her. She has been my neighbour for the past 5 years. I still remember the first time I moved into my apartment, she was the first one to offer me some fresh *Chhole Kulche* that she had cooked that morning. I instantly loved my apartment because of this comfort. I felt at home. As if there was someone to look out for me. Living all by yourself in a foreign country isn't easy.

But did that mean I would let her do whatever she wanted in my home?

My sacred space?

My *garden*?

I always shared food with my neighbours. No matter what I have cooked or even to step out for groceries, I'd always ask if they needed something, out of courtesy. I like doing that.

She looked upset.

I felt the need to apologise. Not sure why, I opened my mouth to apologise but then another voice came into my head. *'This isn't worth your time. If she understands what just happened, you don't have to apologise. If she doesn't, she isn't meant to be in your life.'*

I really wished I had this inner voice, this nice saintly wisdom growing up, but as they say, *'there's no better day than today'* or something like that.

I smiled as she made her way out. I knew I wouldn't get any more 'good food' from her. But more importantly, I would also not get unexpected visits from her and THAT felt like *peace*.

❧

Did I do something right? Maybe many of you reading this don't agree with what I did. That's fine. You don't have to agree. Maybe some of you do agree. That's fine too. It wasn't about the groceries. Or the food.

It was about the attitude.

I didn't feel the need to even explain myself to her. If she had only asked me nicely waiting at the door itself, I would have been more than happy to help her. I understand that some cultures are okay with behaviours like that where one person barges in because they feel it's their home and they feel close to you. But even then, simply asking me if it was okay or can she borrow those things would have made a huge difference.

It is about respect.

It is about considering the other individual.

It is about holding space for another person.

I am Samara. Maybe even you are. Perhaps we all have been in her place at some point in time.

Boundaries may take a conscious assessment and effort to know what's really going on and how one can set them in order to function better and preserve our energies. But if something doesn't feel right, chances are it isn't. My gut told me how to draw a boundary for someone accessing my beautiful home, *my garden.*

If you liked this story and would love to know more about boundaries, subscribe to Kaleidoscope Ezine today!

About the Writer

Arushi Sharma

Arushi is a PhD candidate in Law at Trinity College Dublin and her research work revolves around Data Protection in the financial sector. A full-time law student and a part-time energy worker, she is passionate about teaching and learning. With more than 7 years of experience in healing, she firmly believes in the transformative power of self-reflection and the guidance that each healing offers. Her offerings as a healer and coach help individuals navigate challenges and confidently embrace opportunities.

VI

Finding My Center: The Journey Within

Finding My Center:
The Journey Within

The latter part of 2018 marked a significant shift in my life. I lost my father, and with him, a very important part of my attachment went away. This led to a major change in the way I looked at life. It seemed worthless for a big part of 2019, eventually leading to a slight crack in my marital relationship.

All through this roller coaster ride, I was seeking something, trying to find something, asking people I knew about what is the meaning of this life. My quest took a new meaning when I stumbled upon Isha's Inner Engineering course. It was online, it was structured, and it allowed me to be away from the mundane for a few minutes every day.

The process was long, but it opened a new path for me and gave my search for life and life's meaning a new dimension. In so many years, for the first time, I could just sit and not be perturbed. I used to get affected to the point of crying out silently, but after doing the Shambhavi Mahamudra Kriya, I did feel a connection to something more significant. I could understand the futility of holding onto grudges. I saw meaning and purpose for my life. The whole idea of spirituality, at a very macro level, dawned onto me. It was like a sliver of light amidst the black cloud.

There was a surge of energy, my focus at work increased. I could connect to things in a more meaningful way. The realization of everything being temporary directed me to cement the idea of "letting go". Earlier, I used to hold on to words spoken by people; I used to feel bad about being served later and that too on a smaller plate as compared to my husband, felt perturbed at performing so many rituals. However, once I adopted the mantra of "letting go", all this became very easy. It was like dirt being washed away and I coming out clean and anew.

Have you ever wondered that our world is limited to what we can think about? Thinking is an abstract activity, while it has resulted in new inventions and creative ideas, it has also led to people getting bogged down with it. If the thoughts are not directed inward, they lead to chaos.

During one of my meditations, I chanced upon this insight of "Out of Sight is Out of mind" as in, the world is what we see, hear, feel and think. To explain this, I would like to take you on a small journey. Just imagine – you are in your house and your parents are away in their house. Think about whether they are with you? Do they exist physically? Can you see what they are doing right now when you are cooking or working? The simple answer is "No". Unless you pick up the phone and call them, but then, at that point in time, you are not cooking or working, you are talking to them. During that time, does your work exist, or does your cooking exist?

These questions kept popping into my mind from the time I had done Inner Engineering, yet I wasn't able to understand the depth of the "There is no past or future, the moment is just now". While I was meditating, suddenly, it hit me like a bolt of lightning, "being in the moment" is the only truth. There is no past and no future. It is only me and my inner self; everything else is an illusion that our mind has created. We get attached to illusions, and we suffer when we lose them, we get hurt when our expectations from these illusions are not fulfilled.

Once the above understanding enveloped me like a cloak, the expectation that I had from others significantly decreased. This has ensured that I am able to continue doing things at the same pace even if, a friend didn't respond immediately or my seniors at work didn't appreciate or recognize my contributions. It is not to say, that I don't get perturbed or angry but it has helped me to look at things more objectively and detach myself from the whole situation.

This realization and insight has made me more humble. Earlier I didn't understand what "to surrender" meant. Now, when I have started practising "Letting Go", in a way, I have started surrendering and started to stop worrying too much. This has made me more happy and joyful. I laugh a lot more now.

Reaching this point has been a long process and I am aware that there is a long way to go. In our current situation and life, where we are, it becomes very difficult for us to let go and not get attached. I have learnt to better myself and focus on things that are required to be done at the moment.

Spirituality to me means "being in the moment, letting go and doing everything you do with full attention and to the best of your ability, not worrying too much about the results". There is nothing we came with and there is nothing we will take and go.

This process that I am into is a work in progress and will continue. To find my inner self and be one with it and the power it has, is a long journey and I am enjoying every moment of this journey since I know, there is a beautiful end.

About the Writer

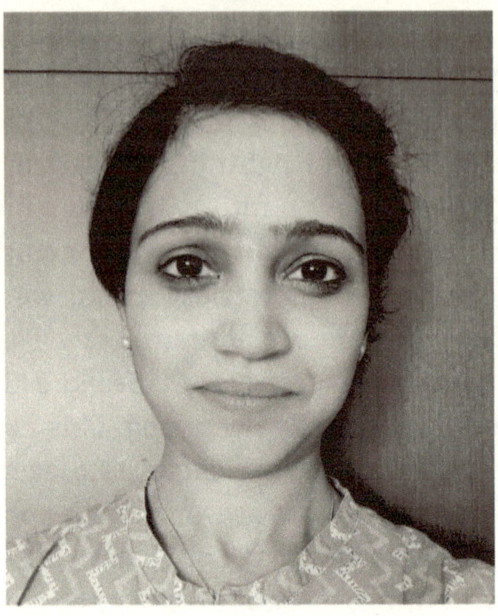

Susmita Shroff

Susmita firmly believes in being a learner throughout life and is passionate about bringing transformation in the lives of teachers and learners. An avid reader and writer, Susmita has been in the education field for the past 10 years and has another 10 years' experience working in the corporate finance sector. She is the Executive Director and Senior Faculty at Teacher Ink. She has been actively involved in teaching and learning audits for schools and has been running the Nursery Teachers' Training (N.T.T) programme for the past seven years through Teacher Ink. Over the period of the past seven years, she has worked with multiple schools as a subject teacher for the primary grades, teaching different subjects and in the capacity of a class teacher as well.

VII

Spirituality: Dark Night or the Awakening

Spirituality:
Dark Night or the Awakening

What is Spirituality? Is it the passing of the "Dark night", or is it "the awakening", or is it just "#Rizz", as the younger generation might call it? There is no standard definition of spirituality. And every individual has their own version of it. Often, it is an experience, a journey that takes you to a much deeper level of self-awareness in many ways.

I cannot point a finger at a time when Spirituality "happened" to me, but I believe its origin lay in the "dark times" of my life. As I navigated through those strenuous times, I found myself being more drawn to tools like meditation and prayer. I felt more drawn to deep dive into the underlying issues, which made me question everything. It was a war between my Left-brain and Right-brain. Nevertheless, as I began to recognize this journey, I started finding peace in chaos. It was then that I realized that in addition to being religious, I was "spiritual" too (another debatable topic).

While I always had an interest in the mystical world, it was this book by Paulo Coelho, *"Brida,"* which motivated me to pursue Tarot.As a teenager, I was quite fascinated by Tarot cards, but I never knew what exactly it was. I started taking online lessons on Udemy, started watching various YouTube videos, and finally bought the Tarot deck & Oracle cards to do practice readings. During this period, I also got Reiki certified. I was determined to go to the root of the issues, identify the triggers, and learn how to best manage the situations around me.

But it was still not enough for me to mature my thoughts on spirituality. I was still in delusion; I was still not able to understand the whys & hows of my life. To this date, it is a struggle. I am still finding my life's purpose. But as I have continued this journey, and made healing a daily habit, I have a better handle on situations that earlier threw me off completely. I now understand what triggers me, how it affects me, and what I should best do to ensure my reactions are not based on ego.

It is pertinent to note that Spirituality is a never-ending journey. For me, it is synonymous with healing. It is more personal & subjective than just being a philosophy.

Spirituality is not a textbook that will give you all the answers, but it will certainly help you realize that the answers to your questions, the resolution to your problem, is within you. All you need to do is, sit with yourself, listen to your intuition, and follow your heart.

Stages of my Spirituality

I would like to break down my experience with Spirituality into the following phases.

1. Denial
2. Coming out of Stupor
3. Acceptance of Denial
4. Acceptance of reality
5. Digestion
6. Healing continues

Denial

Denial for me was not accepting the situation that was present in front of me. My desire to control the outcome did not allow me to see what was real. For a long time, I refused to see my present, to accept the reality.

The grieving period, for me, was losing myself to the situation or circumstances around me. Rather than acknowledging it, I escaped from it. I kept telling myself a different story. This was my defense mechanism that protected me from the shock of the upsetting hardship. This made me delusional, which brings me to the next stage of my spiritual journey.

Coming out of stupor

I have always believed in fairy tale romances, happy endings and all things good. I blame Hollywood! The icing on the cake is the Neptune planet, which seems to have dominated my birth chart for long. While all this has contributed to me being delulu, it is the self-sabotaging behaviour as well, which has been a cherry on top.

The reason I can so comfortably talk about this today is the long and rigorous healing process. As I kept doing the inner work, I slowly but surely came out of the stupor. I started looking at things from a unique perspective, and not through my rose-colored glasses (not sponsored by Ray-Ban!).

When I realized (the hard way) that my never-ending crying was not helping, and there was nothing that I could do to "control" the situation, I finally "surrendered." I surrendered to the higher power. The moment I did that, I eventually started to come out of the state of unconsciousness (metaphorically). This further led to the next stage of "acceptance."

Acceptance of denial

I finally accepted that I had been in denial all this while. That I have not allowed myself to look beyond my limited self. My ego has been winning the battles with my higher self.

I let myself be in this stage for a good amount of time. One key lesson I learnt along the way was that I was never hard on myself. I accepted the truth that I was in denial, and I "forgave" myself. I followed the Hoʻoponopono meditation, which also made me start practicing *self-love*, another opinionated subject that has numerous notions.

Acceptance of reality

Moving on this spiritual path, I began to accept the reality and perceive it as it is now. I acknowledged my present and started being in it. I associate this phase with "The Hanged Man" in the tarot, where I not only learnt to surrender, but also changed my perception.

I paused for this reality to sync in. I gave myself the permission and time to adjust to these changes as they affected me on all levels (emotional, mental, physical & spiritual). I call this phase – "DIGESTION".

Digestion

Change is the only constant in life, and not all of us are given the tools that enable us to adapt to these changes. Hence, always go easy on yourself. I stayed in this phase for a long time too. I ensured that my mind, body and soul were all aligned with this change. I gave myself enough break time, whenever possible, I spent "me-time", practiced self-care, as it was and never is easy.

The Healing Continues

Emotional & spiritual healing is a continued voyage that comes with its own ebbs and flows. I have had days when I am overwhelmed by it, and then there are days when I can't survive without it. But one must go with the flow, and let the healing take its course. It is not necessary to use any tools like Reiki or EFT, even a few minutes of meditation can help you manoeuvre the daily nuances that might trigger you. Having said that, Reiki and EFT help a lot along the way.

Tips to know you are on a spiritual path

In conclusion, below are some tips to know you are on a spiritual path:

a. You stop relating to people you used to, especially the pretentious ones
b. Your social circle is reduced by 50%
c. You are unable to pretend to care
d. You can identify what triggered a particular reaction
e. Your body will stop accepting toxic, processed food
f. You would like to sleep more than usual (particularly if you have sleeping disorders)
g. You will start appreciating me-time
h. Nature will appear more beautiful than usual
a. Gratitude will be more appealing than whining
j. You will certainly be more accepting of love and compassion
k. You will trust your own judgement over other
ax. You understand the meaning of existential crises

This is a long list and can vary from person to person.

Let me conclude by saying that to be spiritual is to embark on a beautiful journey of a deeper connection with oneself and embracing the greater essence of existence.

About the Writer

Neetu Khanna

Hi, I am Neetu, an IT Professional based out of London, and I love what I do. When not working (and not doing the dishes/hoover), I love to spend time with my daughter, watch Netflix, and read a book. I am a sunset lover, a dog lover, and I value meaningful conversations. I have a very open and unconventional approach to life. You will always see me with a smile on my face.

VIII

The Inner Odyssey: Journey of Self-Love

The Inner Odyssey:
Journey of Self-Love

*"Nobody will protect you from your suffering. You can't cry it away or eat it away or starve it away or walk it away or punch it away or even therapy it away. It's just there, and you have to survive it. You have to endure it. You have to live through it and love it and move on and be better for it and run as far as you can in the direction of your best and happiest dreams across the bridge that was built by your own desire to heal. ~**Cheryl Strayed**"*

These words are precious – they are insightful and completely summarize what happens when you are healing from within. It is a journey and all journeys take time, guidance can come from therapy, journaling and other forms of help, however, the endurance of it is yours to own and heal.

However, there is hope - Pain is given, but suffering is your choice – the intensity of it, the extent of it and how long it will last. This brings me to the core of the issue – why do we want to suffer? Why do we prolong the agony? Is it because we feel we deserve to suffer; we must do due repentance and feel guilty enough? If you have deliberately, intentionally harmed or hurt someone, then by all means, you do need to understand your behaviour and suffer through it. Even then, suffering alone is not enough, the recipient of your actions needs your apologies, explanations and needs to forgive you. That brings me to the core of your actions and suffering – self-love.

Many interpretations of this phrase are available and are understood in varying degrees, maybe even according to what suits the person. When you really understand and believe in self-love, you will understand that it means emptying yourself of as much toxicity, negativity and suffering as possible. If this means you lower your ego and ask for forgiveness, make amends and atone for the hurt inflicted by you, so be it. The ultimate goal is to become empty again – to fill yourself with purity so you can make healthy re-starts.

Self-love is not indulgence, self-pity or blaming others for your suffering. Quite the opposite. It is attained after you stop indulging yourself childishly, after you acknowledge your weaknesses and vulnerabilities and understand how you make your own self-hurting decisions. Self-love is actually attained when you free yourself from all constraints and boundaries including the ones created by you such as being a victim.

It is not as frivolous as retail therapy, going to a spa or relaxing in a soap-filled tub. Those are relaxing but do not fill you with joy that lasts a lifetime. These are temporary assuages that you make-believe, as the real work needed for self-help is hard. It means facing your own demons, fears, insecurities and accepting that maybe you alone created your suffering. Nevertheless, when you forgive yourself, understanding why, what emotions and what perceptions led you to create a hardened image of yourself, you start moving towards self-love.

There is another myth that when people start feeling self-love, it comes at the cost of enjoying their solitude or walking away from toxic places or people etc. Whether that happens as a natural corollary is a consequence but not a necessity to feel self-love. What may happen instead is that as you become more self-contained and understanding of yourself, you become your own best friend. You may choose to spend more time with yourself but not at the cost of isolating yourself. You need to be approving and liking of your own company and may also choose to be with others. As you become more self-contained, you move away from the drama of situations and people by not letting it affect you too much. However, self-love does not come at the cost of unloving others or not feeling compassionate — quite the opposite.

Neither is self-love contingent on your materialistic success, how well you are doing at work or the kind of social circles and friends you accumulate. It just comes when you accept your imperfections, your ups and downs and possibly realize your weaknesses. If being reactive and overly emotional is your weakness, you calmly accept it and decide to be aware of it. Question it lovingly and get to the root of it – maybe it comes from not being given enough attention or feeling overwhelmed sooner than others. We all have our thresholds, though we can always work towards self-improvement. We can stretch our thresholds if that is what life requires from us. However, do take breaks, take a deep breath and walk in nature when your heart and soul cry for it. These are its coping mechanisms so that you can come back to a space of calm and peace again, ready to face life head-on.

Not hearing your inner voice or your body's call of distress is ignoring yourself, and that comes at an expense. Trying to prove yourself comes from low self-worth, and the world outside will demand more work from us as that is their way. By all means, fully participate in this, work like the world does, and do not resist or reject it. The difference that comes when you are filled with self-love is you will know when to withdraw as well. Mentally, physically and emotionally. Understanding that this is the way the world needs me, but this is not who I am. I am merely appearing the way others can accommodate me, but I am a vast expanse of so much more. Again, that does not amount to more achievements, toils and hard work – just accepting that the inner expansiveness allows you to 'travel' astrally and figuratively beyond the confines of the physical boundaries of your present life.

Accept and appreciate you are so much more than is available to the physical senses, that is the true and pure consequence of self-love.

About the Writer

Nandita Kaushik

Nandita Kaushik is a life coach, author, tarot reader, reiki master and is trained in many coaching tools and methods. Passionate about writing, she delves into deep spiritual concepts and brings more clarity and simplicity to life and living. She has a corporate experience of almost 30 years in marketing services and brand communication. Nandita's latest book "Rediscover your Midlife Mojo" has been an instant attention grabber and has hooked the interest of people - both young and old.

IX
Tarot Speak for November 2024

Tarot Speak
for November 2024

Aries (Mar 21 – Apr 19)

Aries, you are in for a fast-paced and energetic month. The Knight of Swords indicates that you may be rushing forward with determination, but it's important to avoid acting without thinking things through.

- **Career & Finances:** You'll likely feel the urge to push ahead aggressively in your career. You may need to act quickly on decisions, but be careful not to rush too fast. Opportunities will come, but ensure you are prepared and informed. Financially, this is a time to make smart moves without being impulsive.
- **Love & Relationships:** In relationships, you might feel impatient or eager for progress. Whether single or in a relationship, try to balance your drive with compassion. Be mindful of how your fast-paced energy affects others.
- **Health:** Your energy levels are high this month but don't forget to rest. Overexerting yourself could lead to burnout, so take breaks when needed.

Taurus (Apr 20 – May 20)

Taurus, November is a time of giving and receiving. The Six of Pentacles encourages balance in your financial dealings and personal relationships.

- **Career & Finances:** At work, you may find yourself in a position to help others or to be helped. Collaborations could prove fruitful, and sharing resources or knowledge will benefit you in the long run. Financially, there could be unexpected assistance or gifts coming your way.
- **Love & Relationships:** In love, you may feel more generous or receive kindness from your partner or loved ones. If single, this is a good time to give back to your community or loved ones, as this positive energy will attract meaningful connections.
- **Health:** Balance is key for your health this month. If you've been neglecting self-care, now is the time to give yourself the attention you need.

Gemini (May 21 – Jun 20)

For Gemini, November brings a sense of completion and fulfillment. The World card suggests that something important in your life is coming full circle.

- **Career & Finances:** In your career, you may finally achieve a goal you've been working towards. It's a time to celebrate your success and think about new challenges. Financially, you'll likely feel secure, and there may be a sense of abundance around you.
- **Love & Relationships:** In relationships, you may experience harmony and unity. If in a relationship, this card suggests a deep connection and shared understanding. If single, this could be a time when you feel content and complete within yourself.
- **Health:** Your health looks stable and strong. Any long-standing issues may find resolution, and you'll feel more in control of your well-being.

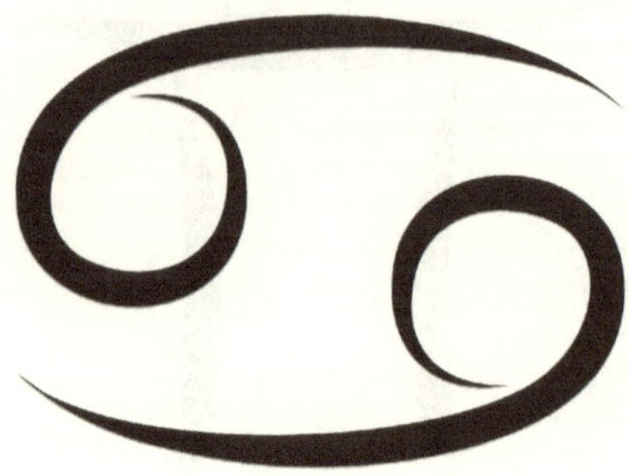

Cancer (Jun 21 – Jul 22)

Cancer, the Nine of Cups brings a month of emotional satisfaction and contentment. You're likely to feel fulfilled in various areas of your life.

- **Career & Finances:** Professionally, things are likely to go your way. A project you've been working on could reach a satisfying conclusion, and you'll feel proud of your achievements. Financially, you're in a comfortable position, and it's a good time to enjoy the rewards of your hard work.
- **Love & Relationships:** In love, you'll experience joy and closeness with your partner or loved ones. If single, you'll feel content with where you are and optimistic about future romantic possibilities.
- **Health:** Your emotional well-being is strong this month, which positively impacts your physical health. You'll feel in tune with yourself, which will lead to overall wellness.

Leo (Jul 23 – Aug 22)

Leo, November is a month for introspection. The Hermit urges you to step back from the hustle and focus on inner growth.

- **Career & Finances:** In your career, you may need to take some time to reflect on your path and decisions. This is a good period for planning and realigning your goals. Financially, be cautious and thoughtful with your spending. Saving for the future is a wise move.
- **Love & Relationships:** You might feel the need for space in your relationships. This isn't a time to rush into decisions or changes in love; instead, reflect on what you truly want. If single, enjoy the peace of solitude and self-discovery.
- **Health:** Focus on mental and emotional well-being this month. Meditation, mindfulness, or simply spending quiet time with yourself will bring balance to your health.

Virgo (Aug 23 – Sep 22)

Virgo, the Five of Swords signals challenges and potential conflict in November. You may need to navigate tricky situations, especially around communication.

- **Career & Finances:** In your professional life, you could face competition or disagreements. Stay calm and think carefully before responding to any conflicts. Financially, this is a time to avoid unnecessary risks and protect your resources.
- **Love & Relationships:** In love, misunderstandings or arguments could arise. Be patient and try to communicate openly to avoid further tension. If single, take care not to get involved in unnecessary drama.
- **Health:** Stress might take a toll on your health, so focus on relaxation and managing any anxiety. Take time to recharge and avoid situations that drain your energy.

Libra (Sep 23 – Oct 22)

Libra, you might feel trapped or restricted in November. The Eight of Swords indicates that you could be holding yourself back, but there is a way forward.

- **Career & Finances**: In your career, you may feel stuck or unsure of how to move ahead. Remember, many of these barriers are self-imposed. Break free from limiting thoughts and trust that you can find solutions. Financially, be cautious and avoid making hasty decisions.
- **Love & Relationships**: In love, you might feel restricted or confused about where things are headed. Take time to reflect on what's holding you back from experiencing fulfillment in your relationships.
- **Health:** Mentally, this month may bring feelings of stress or anxiety. Practicing mindfulness and talking things through with someone you trust can help ease these emotions.

Scorpio (Oct 23 – Nov 21)

Scorpio, The Devil card brings focus on temptations and attachments. November asks you to be mindful of unhealthy habits or relationships.

- **Career & Finances:** At work, you may feel stuck in a toxic environment or over-committed. It's important to recognize any unhealthy dynamics and start working towards breaking free. Financially, be cautious of overspending or falling into old patterns that don't serve you.
- **Love & Relationships:** In love, be mindful of power struggles or unhealthy attachments. If you're in a relationship, this is a time to address any imbalances. If single, make sure you're not seeking connections that limit your personal growth.
- **Health:** Watch out for addictive behaviours or negative patterns that could affect your health. This is a good time to focus on breaking free from anything that doesn't support your well-being.

Sagittarius (Nov 22 – Dec 21)

Sagittarius, November is your time to shine. The Queen of Wands encourages you to embrace your confidence and take bold actions.

- **Career & Finances:** In your career, your leadership qualities will stand out. You'll have the opportunity to take charge and inspire others. Financially, this is a good time to invest in something you're passionate about, as your confidence will guide you towards success.
- **Love & Relationships:** In relationships, you'll feel charismatic and attractive, drawing positive attention. If single, you're likely to meet someone who matches your fiery energy. If in a relationship, expect more passion and excitement.
- **Health:** Your health looks vibrant, but keep an eye on maintaining balance. Channel your high energy into activities that support both your physical and mental well-being.

Capricorn (Dec 22 – Jan 19)

Capricorn, the Ace of Cups promises a month of emotional renewal. This card indicates new beginnings, especially in your emotional life.

- **Career & Finances:** In your career, you might start a new project or develop stronger connections with colleagues. This is a good time for collaboration and nurturing professional relationships. Financially, expect a positive shift, with growth opportunities.
- **Love & Relationships:** In love, this card signals new emotional beginnings. If you're single, a new romance could be on the horizon. If in a relationship, you may feel a deepening of your emotional bond.
- **Health:** Emotionally, you'll feel renewed and more in touch with your feelings. This will positively affect your overall health, bringing a sense of calm and well-being.

Aquarius (Jan 20 – Feb 18)

Aquarius, the King of Swords urges you to take a rational and analytical approach to life this month. It's a time for clear thinking and decisive actions.

- **Career & Finances:** In your career, use your intellect to make strategic decisions. You may be called upon to take a leadership role or mentor others. Financially, being logical and calculated with your investments or expenses will pay off.
- **Love & Relationships:** In relationships, you'll need to communicate clearly and set boundaries where necessary. Avoid getting caught up in emotions, and focus on what's logical and fair.
- **Health:** Your mental health will benefit from structure and discipline. Take a methodical approach to any health concerns and avoid letting stress build-up.

Pisces (Feb 19 – Mar 20)

Pisces, the Two of Cups brings harmony and connection into your life. This is a month for deepening bonds and enjoying companionship.

- **Career & Finances:** In your career, you'll find that working with others brings success. Collaborations will thrive, and you'll feel supported by your colleagues. Financially, partnerships or joint ventures may bring good results.
- **Love & Relationships:** In love, this is a beautiful time for relationships. If in a relationship, you'll feel more connected than ever. If single, someone special could enter your life, sparking a meaningful connection.
- **Health:** Emotionally, you'll feel balanced and at peace, which will positively affect your physical health. Focus on nurturing your emotional bonds, as this will uplift your overall well-being.

About the Writer

Meetu Sehgal

Meetu Sehgal is a Personal Transformation and Emotional Wellness Coach, EFT Trainer, Tarot Reader, Author, Reiki Grandmaster and Counselling Psychologist. With more than 15 years of experience in her field, she has been passionately working with individuals, helping them resolve health, wealth and relationship challenges through coaching. Meetu Sehgal is an MBA graduate from Delhi University and also holds a Masters in Psychology. Passionate about writing and spirituality, she has blended both in her work, which has helped hundreds of people around the world find peace within themselves. Her latest book, "Happy Inside Out", is a definitive guide to understanding and handling emotions and moods.

ABOUT EZINE KALEIDOSCOPE

In this new age, the definition and meaning of the word 'Spirituality' has become varied and is often misconstrued with fear, religion and a monk sitting in meditation on a lonely Himalayan mountain.

But spirituality is much beyond this faulty image. It is an inherent part of who we are. Because truly, we are spiritual being having a human experience.

The purpose of Ezine Kaleidoscope is to bring the true essence of spirituality to our readers and make it so accessible that it doesn't feel like an alien overwhelming concept anymore. Our aim is to make it a part of everyone's everyday life.

> *"If every living moment can be full of awareness, there will be joy and bliss in the world*
>
> *-Meetu Sehgal"*

Ezine Kaleidoscope's journey began in November 2010 as a journey towards spirituality, awareness and making the spiritual tools accessible to all in a simple understandable manner.

It is our vision and mission to create awareness and remove the element of fear from spirituality and all things related. It is vested in light and that's what we want to bring to the life of everyone who reads us.

Know more about us

Website: ezinekaleidoscope.com
Email: info@ezinekaleidoscope.com
Instagram: @Ezine.Kaleidoscope
Facebook: www.facebook.com/ezineKaleidoscope